BEFORE THE

CITY

For Marisa Shuman,
ua mau ke ea o ka aina i ka pono,
Aloha nō,
Kirby Wright

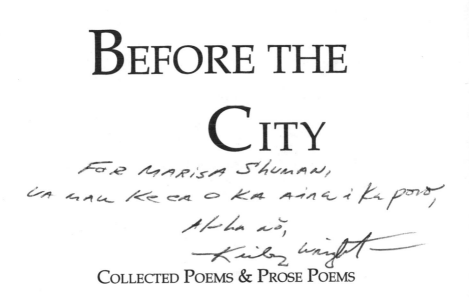

COLLECTED POEMS & PROSE POEMS

KIRBY WRIGHT

FOREWORD BY DANIEL BOURNE

Lemon Shark Press
San Diego, CA
www.lemonsharkpress.com

Book design: Lemon Shark Press
Cover art: *La Danse de Nu* by Kristof

Printed in the USA

ISBN 0-9741067-0-4

San Diego, CA
www.lemonsharkpress.com

Acknowledgments

My gratitude to the editors of the following journals, magazines, presses, reviews, and anthologies in which some of these poems and prose poems first appeared: *Artful Dodge, The Bar Harbor Times, Black Bear Review, Blackmail Press, Blue Fifth Review, Blue Mesa Review, Branches Quarterly, The Cape Rock, Chaminade Literary Review, Coe Review, Cold Mountain Review, The Drunken Boat, The Fairfield Review, Fox Cry Review, Friends of Acadia Journal, The Green Tricycle, Hawai'i Review, Horizon Magazine, Ink Magazine, In Posse Review, Into the Teeth of the Wind, Ludlow Press, Maryland Review, Megaera Magazine, Molokai Advertiser-News, The Ohio Poetry Review, Palo Alto Review, the-phone-book.com, Pierian Springs, Plainsongs, Poetry Magazine, The Prose Poem: An International Journal, Red Booth Review, Red Rock Review, Reed Magazine, Santa Clara Review, Shampoo Poetry, sidereality, Slant: A Journal of Poetry, Slipstream, Stirring, Taj Mahal Review, Thunder Sandwich, Toyon Literary Journal, Trestle Creek Review, Trout Journal, UC Review, The Wayne Literary Review, The West Wind Review, Wisconsin Review, Words on a Wire, Writers' Forum,* and *Writers Monthly*.

The poems "Messages from La Frontera" and "Aloha, Lili'uokalani" won the Robert Browning Society Award in successive years. "Life Extension" won the Ann Fields Poetry Prize. "At Il Fornaio, San Francisco" was among a suite of poems that received the Academy of American Poets Award. "Nútungktatoka" was nominated for the Pushcart Prize.

I wish to thank the poets Frances Mayes, Myung Mi Kim, Gillian Conoley, and Daniel J. Langton for their encouragement and helpful critiques of my work. I am also grateful for the Arts Council Silicon Valley Fellowship in Poetry, which gave me the time to complete this collection.

For Harold & June
On their 50th

Contents

Foreword

Smart-mouthed and serious, sometimes bawdy and usually wise, the poems in Kirby Wright's *Before the City* remind me of the paintings of Peter Brueghal, swarming with the large and small incidents of life. As one of the first editors to publish his poetry (the loopy portrait of the artist as a young man entitled "The Mark of the Ass"), I am only chagrined by not getting to publish other such gems as "Quake" or "The Architects," poems that show—in the hands of someone as engaged and as deft as Wright—how surrealism, lyricism and human commentary go hand and hand. It is no surprise that Wright's poetry indeed stems from the geographic landscapes where he has lived—Hawaii and California, particularly.

Austere and lush in turn, Wright's poetry notices both a roadside ironwood tree's knowledge of "the meaning of alone" as well as the way in which night-blooming cereus spreads itself open to the circling moths. Whether bemoaning the merchandising of Hawaii or chronicling the twilight constantly coming on in people's lives, Wright's poetry certainly has some important assertions as we head off into a new century: "I am certain we are shorter than the truth," he states in "Dining with Your Headshot," or "you can't move something without risking history," he says in "Ironwood."

You can tell Wright wants his poetry to reconfigure the world so that we can better see its subterranean connections—and thereby better evaluate what is truly important: "Funny how our pink roses resemble backyard rags—toilet paper caught on branches," he writes at the end of "Transformations in Northern California." Wright also wants to celebrate the truly important aspects of being human—no matter how seemingly slight. His description of the man who "smells macaroni and cheese on a neighbor's stove" and "is relieved their day has ended" indeed rises up to give me a quiet yet powerful image of the poet going about the poet's work— doing the job only writers (like Wright) still realize the need to do.

Daniel Bourne, Editor, *Artful Dodge*

Before the City

Haven't seen you in a week.

Today is Tuesday.

The Dutch Elm shivers on the front lawn.

A U—Haul waits at the curb.

These houses that watch me are coffins.

The suburbs are a Cold War painting.

Neighbors stand at windows and in doorways to their own graves.

I press Rewind and Play, see us over.

Beyond glass, past the shutters, you are safe at a distance.

I never intended the old man to break through my eyes.

A UPS truck circles the block.

In the city I'll rent what belongs to my father.

The face of his fridge rusts.

He says I failed in life.

I pack firecrackers to warn me of fires.

I know I will die alone.

Life Extension

With modern medicine, isn't all life artificial?
Wonder drugs make us artifacts, might someday
Preserve us longer than Methuselah, the antediluvian.
Walt Disney's still alive in a cryogenic sense,
His skin as blue as Matterhorn snow. It's a wonder
I survived babyhood after three convulsions,
Thank god Mrs. Tamura held down my tongue with a
Spoon. Lives keep extending, making postwar babies
The envy of their prewar parents. What about pets?
That cat down the street isn't breathing the way he did
Last week. Must be his diet. Some owners give their
Dogs and cats Life Extension, either in powder or tablets.
After powder, Grandma's Chihuahua wants to be bounced on
My knee like a baby. My vet says animal longevity can't be
Predicted. He's right, especially when you consider the
Omnipresent threat of traffic. In the human world,
Orchestra conductors live the longest—something about
Commanding with hands, making faces, waving a wand
In front of trained musicians. I doubt train conductors live
As long, although their approach whistle might resemble
A note blown from an archangel's trumpet. My uncle wanted
Taps played over his grave. Will I be buried with
Cuff links polished? Gold watch strapped to my wrist?
Saint Michael on a swimmer's chain around my neck?

A classmate I once loved keeps getting posthumous
Awards in my quarterly bulletin, this one for
Lifetime Achievement. It's as if she never really left.
Our lives keep overlapping in Alumni Notes, even though
In high school we hardly touched. Sometimes I break out
The tarot deck, work it like a Geiger counter—
Detecting spiritual fallout, measuring ethereal
Particles, interpreting her half-life, trying to kiss a ghost.

Tea

Tea on the table
Warms my hands
In the hours

Before words
Leak to stain
The bone-white cup.

Construction Residential

Next door is tear down, concrete cracking
Like eggshells, killing old driveway. No warning,
Just hard hats arriving in trucks, jackhammering
Under the Dutch Elm. Neighbors pay for
Circular pathway, entrances and exits moving
Clockwise. One-day job. Men sharpen shovels,
Prepare the rubble. Bodies are orchestra of
Hands on tools, performing destruction.
How much of construction begins with destroy?
Are these the same neighbors I asked for one cup
Of sugar, two eggs for a cake, to split the cost
Of our fence? Metal shapes the August ground.
Sweat. Heads tilt back for soda, water.
Contractor pounds stake with rubber mallet.
Hired jeans lean into contract, reveal under-
Pants with every bend. Residential deal. Mixer
Boasting *South Bay Concrete* backs up, grunts,
Belly full of wet cement. Earth waits for flood,
Surrounded by braces. Everything's production—
Pour, pour, pour. Gray pools form, get shaped,
Are left to harden, cure, become top of coffin.
Concrete came fast, much earlier than expected.
Below surfaces, can earth still remember
Where it came from, birthplace, its own grave?

Observations from Oceanside

The beach is nearly deserted.
Sandpipers scuttle,

Then stab the wet sand
With beaks.

A jogger appears
Then disappears

Into a mirage
Rising off the strand.

The day smells industrial.
A power plant to the south

Sends black plumes
Out of its tower.

A man paddles a boogie board
Through the shallows.

Offshore, a gray destroyer
Treads water. It seems

As harmless as
A bathtub toy.

The war is a distant thing
Where men, women,

And children die
Beyond the bent horizon.

Rain after a Dry Spell

The promised storm has come.
The weathermen are ecstatic.

Rain washes the bare limbs
Of the poplar.

Gopher mounds
Flatten and melt.

A distant eucalyptus
Sways in the hills.

The propane tank
Greens as if freshly painted.

The ground releases
The burnt grass smell of drought.

This change complicates matters;
Now the dead are expected

To be more than ornamental.
They are expected to recover.

The tumbleweeds are amused.
They roll and spin

In the wind
Like unsupervised children.

Loops of razored wire
Sparkle on the fence line.

A white egret lands in the field.
The earth shivers with life.

The Roses are Fifteen

Your purchase? Fifteen red longstems roped by white string. You bought at noon, at the border where roses grow like weeds with many thorns, thorns threatening your hands in this desert heat.

Roses struggle out of the dust of my land, senoritã, and I pick these weeds because you buy them instead of the flowers on your side. You want the discount. But there is trouble with my blossoms—they wilt after you pass the checkpoint. Your guard waved you home after smelling their innocence in your hands, but my roses die even as you drive because my sweat was not enough to keep them alive. Buds droop in clumps, refusing life beyond the border. Thorns are stilettos on the stems, blades jutting from twisted frames.

My supply? Over forty bunches. You took the biggest. I said it looked like a dozen, take them. I lied. I let you have the extras because I knew you would be happy with a bargain. You made the deal. I only hoped the thorns would not cut badly, you waiting patiently for the buds to open, you not believing a newborn could die in your arms with no warning at all. You must watch surrendering petals drip off the buds: they bleed across the table and spill, staining your floor.

You purchased my flowers. Now live with them as their romance drains. My roses seduced and deceived you. Careful not to wound yourself as you pull fifteen stems from the dead water, one by one.

Messages from La Frontera

in memory of César Chávez

I. Tijuana

Miguel, why is it always cities that separate us?
My memories walk the cracked cobblestones
Fronting the Jai Alai Palace. Our eyes burned in
The winter smog of Mescal City. Do you remember
The uniforms at every corner of Revolution Boulevard,
How the Federale threesomes prodded beggars along
With the tips of their guns? We strolled past
The Mexico-or-Bust souvenir booth
Run by a toothless man with a broken mule.
Amigo! the shopkeepers called, *Welcome, friend!*
Their pinatas exposed fragile candy bellies
To glass cases lined with stilettos and Rambo knives.
I can still smell the white corn sizzling
Over coals on the vendor's portable stove.
Here, you said, *everything is portable,*
Everything moves for a price. Tourists learned
Pity in the streets, between the morning striptease
In Bambi Club and sunset margaritas at
Tijuana Tilly's. I recall the black-and-white
Picture taken in the Long Bar after the tequila,
The lime, and the salted glasses—we used Corona
To chase the sting from our lips. Mariachis
Asked to play. *How much for a song?*

Four dollars, amigo, their leader said, his thumb
Curved down. *Begin!* I said, then to the bartender,
Uno mas, por favor, just one more round.
I still hear those violins, guitars, and trumpets play.
The bar took my reflection into its fun house mirror
Guarding the exit. I looked like a gringo, a drunk.
I told the girl outside I have no dollars, only pesos,
Maybe two thousand pesos in clumsy change
And paper, paper stained with the faces
Of forgotten leaders. *Sorry, no pesos,* she said.
She marched to the boulevard where her boy
Washed windshields with his one good arm,
Washing glass that was already clean.
Miguel, remember watching the men?
How they gathered in front of liquor stores
Drinking mescal from caramel-colored bottles,
Mouths working toward the dead worm
Waiting on the bottom. *Let them drink,*
You said, *let them dream.* You imagined
Our palm trees rising like rows of arrows, pointing
To the moon in the purple dust above San Diego.
I left you at the border checkpoint
With only a picture, a handshake, and a smile.
It was the same smile I gave so easily in the bar.
I told the dark woman hustling the rows of traffic

I had no money. She took my last three dollars
And dropped a ceramic Santa in the back of my jeep.
I looked back, Miguel, but you were gone.
Ahead, the moon was an eyelash drifting north.

II. The Border

Miguel, U.S. helicopters patrol the marshes
Between countries. These are the wetlands,
The land of endangered species. The war begins.
Helicopter blades cut the night to heartbeats.
Searchlights slice the darkness to ribbons.
Greyhound buses move out of the southern desert
Up Interstate 5 with cargoes of souvenirs and tourists.
The North Star shines like a planet.
A burned-out Dodge is held in the web of fence.
A shadow bends through an elliptical hole
Cut in the wire to allow a body to pass.
In Imperial Beach on the American side,
Condominium owners worry
About fair market value as spotlights
Ignite California's share of Heaven.
Never run when the moon is full, you warned.
The moon is a sliver. Lines form behind the holes.
Most make the sign of the cross under the stars.

Tongues measure the wind, voices held by wire.
Halogen spotlights work like lasers.
A grandmother calls, *Migra! La Migra!*
When the green-and-white INS vans attack.
The vans collect the slow like cattle,
Like so many heads of cattle. The war goes on.
How many voices are silenced by wire?
Who speaks where the holes are cut?
Miguel, all that your people carry
Is held in their mouths.

III. North County

In the beach towns of northern
San Diego County, the phalanx of hands
Work the leaves of vegetable, fruit, and flower.
Fingers reach into the dirt, pulling at things
To fill the empty places in baskets in boxes.
Let them work, you said, *let them heal.*
Miguel, do you work this field of strawberries
Filled with hills of harvesting crates?
Do you search for the small red prize,
Your back curving down around your heart?
There is always another harvest.
Always the bending armies.

Always more shadows needed.

Blood comes cheap from the south, as cheap as

The bouquets your niños sell at intersections.

La familia spends days hiding

Between the rows, bending in delicate places,

Arrested in fields bordering the freeway.

Miguel, who will speak for faces without voices?

It is a silence that kills.

Last night I saw the Southern Cross

Suspended over the waves.

In the land of malaria and cardboard walls

That fringe these cities,

The dead are buried quietly

Under the swollen moon.

Van Gogh Vision

1.

Hear helicopter? she asks.

Not helicopter, I say,

Just fan carving

Our morning, cutting

Dreams from their moorings.

Birds on front lawn

Retreat to the Dutch Elm.

2.

Inside sculptured head of

Van Gogh on library lawn

Is nest. When chicks hatched,

When they flew off

Through Van Gogh's eyes,

They became visions

Feathering into blue.

Winter at Oceanside Beach, California

Santa Anas carry the scent of sage
Out from the desert.

Tumbleweeds reverse directions,
Roll west with the sun.

The sea today is blue and cold
Yet full of hidden treasures.

Where is the ring she lost
Playing in the shallows?

Boats are frozen offshore—
Their captains harvest

Fins and claws
Using nets and poles.

Onshore, a man hooks a snapper,
Smiles like a father

When the flesh is beached.
A girl's laugh is answered

By a seagull's cry.
A black helicopter sails by,

Disappears into the smog.
A grandmother is a child again

Chasing her granddaughter
Over the dirty blond shore.

Broken waves recede,
Exposing the bones of our future.

Smog Check in Sunnyvale

$19.95 isn't such a bad deal for my biennial
Inspection, especially with a chance to sun
Myself in white chair while waiting for emission
Approval from Smog Man. It's somewhere
Between lounging at outdoor bar and waiting inside
Doctor's office, without margarita or magazine
In striking distance. Coke machine beckons.
Only ten minutes more, Smog Man says.
Nissan ahead of me runs in neutral with hood open,
Exposing what makes it tick. Detector's up tailpipe—
Anal tool measuring carbon dioxide, monoxide,
Hydrocarbons. I sit in exhausted air. This might be
My final smog. Nissan chokes, gasping for oxygen.
You're next, Smog Man says, records my serial
Number on dash. Everything's clipboard, red ballpoint,
Carbon copies, pushing down hard. I leave chair
During engine hook up to smog machine. Water and
Compressed air share a metal box around the corner,
25¢ gets you 2 minutes, your choice of elements.
Phone sounds. Mechanic bending over Honda
Responds, slave to rings, rent, bimonthly paycheck.
Honda's bumper instructs, *Plant a Tree, Cool the World.*
Dissembling engine—that compact's in for a bum thermo—

Stat, guilty of overheating, steaming the planet.
Lucifer in the machinery? Strange how minor things
Seem to riot, corrupt major functions, freeze the
Synchronous wheels in place. *You fail,* Smog Man says,
Signs his name in red on the inspection report.
My problem's an overabundance of hydrocarbons.
Some parts speak a different language, challenge
Their assignments, break down mortal orders to go.

At Il Fornaio, San Francisco

Inside Il Fornaio, a sparrow joins me
At the marble table. Sour chirp. Wants
My pumpkin muffin, a sip of espresso, then

To be let out. Overhead heaters crackle,
Brand name, *Sunpak*. Behind glass, soggy
Plaza. Drizzle. Umbrellas sprout—black

Mushrooms at the corners. First day of
Spring. Two women guide a dolly stacked
With cardboard boxes: one pushes, the other

Balances. Sign says, *No Parking 2 a.m. to
6 a.m. Street Cleaning*. Wet cars chase one
Another south on Battery. I drop a crumb of

Muffin. A man with cigarette frowns by,
Walking face, facing fading needs.
What we come to expect becomes limited.

Fear triggers the minimal. Dreams diffuse,
Transfuse the violet sky. Do you own an
Umbrella? Carry the morning paper?

Let a briefcase swing at your knees? The
Plaza fountain spurts across fabricated
Rock. Recycling water show. Tortured river.

This fountain secretly feeds the heavens?
Most gather at crosswalks, waiting for traffic
To stop. Want permission to walk, to disappear

Into red-bricked offices. The sparrow chirps,
Begging for pumpkin, but the muffin's gone.
The bird flies off. Evaporation's endless.

Quake

The city cracks

                In unexpected places,
Forcing angels up
Into the smog.

"It's The Big One!"
The shock jock jams
Into the air waves,
His baritone a 6
On the Richter scale.

The day before,
Dogs and cats left their homes
For parts unknown.
Birds watched from wires
Like officers on a battlefield.

The day after,
The TV preacher
Who ran for President
Threatens to become
An Old Testament prophet.

"We've got hurricanes, floods,

　　Earthquakes, and fires," he warns,

Then asks for $350,000 in 30 minutes.

"That's over ten grand a minute," he says,

　　"Start phoning it in."

The angels fly east

Over the desert,

Blaring their trumpets.

A snake blinks in the shadow of wings.

The Gallery Director

The skin of the gallery director is soft. But his muscles know the strain of production. He smokes in an alley adjacent to The Minotaur Gallery in Carmel. Fog veils the coast. His smoke rises south of Dolores. Streets here resist numbers— they are defined by landmarks, intersections, corners.

He has retired from Broadway with tastes for rehearsals, hors d'oeuvres, and starving actors. His face is not unlike yesterday's or the days before. His vision is no longer curtains—SOLD lifts the soul. The goal is contracts, TRWs, payment plans for the middle class.

"I would go back," he whispers to his two-foot tall Diana. "I would go back, for the right offer." She is Goddess of the Hunt. The gallery director rotates the pedestal, spins so her breasts will face the entrance. He once rallied the stage, motivated troupes for opening nights. His passion for directing purposed his bones. "Why didn't I make it?" the gallery director asks. "Damn know-it-all playwrights," he says shaking his head.

He allows wonder. He opens his stage to the museum stroll of strangers. But the salesman inside suffers. The gallery director knows tourists are killing time, shopping for the least expensive of the expensive art and restaurants, murdering vacations among the Torrey pines. Every afternoon, he sees tickets fluttering on windshields along Ocean Avenue.

His actors? Nudes erupting from blocks of Lucite and bronze. There's life-size Odysseus. Poseidon blushes. The gallery director checks lighting, rearranges his pantheon in the morning hours. He aims his fan at Theseus On His Knees. Glass and metal bodies bend, twist torsos, spill shadows under the halogen moons.

Community Garden

Love sometimes feeds off hate, for grounding.
Tomato, a fruit, rhymes with potato, gets served as
A vegetable. Go down to your Community Garden,
You'll see how red rots. Lazy gardeners, once full
Of good intentions, abandon what they started.
Ignore is a form of hatred—probably makes a
Terrible parent. Ripe begs harvest, wants eaten.
Japanese cucumbers are sweeter than expected.
Woman wheelbarrows yellow squash over
Asphalt to car. Man wearing safari hat bicycles
Down rows of corn. Birds in pumpkin patch
Cross wings, pray for rain or man-made sprinkles
From hoses equipped with shower nozzles.
What happens when hoses can't reach your heart?
Rectangular plots. Red shines through green vine.
Swiss chard's making a comeback. Love ripens, brings
Fruition, tests soil for power. Responsibility threatens
Vitality, attraction, spontaneous combustion; reverses
Your sexual motion. To love then hate is typic mixture,
Convinces tomato it's vegetable. The raspberries are
Experiencing a second coming, they're the optimists of
The garden. Tomatoes keep rotting. Everything firms
Then softens in tragic garden. Gardening destroys things
Slowly, fakes affection, weakens roots and branches.

A grandfather waters his carrots. Attitudes bloom.
The artichokes need cutting before they become flowers.
Zucchini rests like fat baby on bed, content. Grandpa
Stoops to water, conquers drought. Sun blazes, smiles
Realizing this version of Community Garden will
Come, go, be forgotten, leave seeds behind for children.

The Architects

1.

I bang on door

Of warehouse converted to home.

The steel slides up.

Inside, a gathering of architects.

Hands caress champagne glasses.

Hats and Dockers in August.

I enter incongruous, in shorts.

The walls are quartz.

The door chains down.

Host nods from the porte-cochere—he's

Introducing his umbrella

To the senior partner.

Hostess, a Pacific Heights princess,

Breaks bread in the kitchen.

Candlelight tickles her quiche.

She plucks cans of Tuscan clams

Off a graphite shelf.

It is sunset, but it seems much later.

The CEO cruises by in suspenders.

2.

Singles mingle—repartee
Spiced with hors d'oeuvres.

The divorced swim with the married.
The married swim with the single.
Host's ex swills a Volcano.
Speakers speak Motown and Beatles.
I choke on my third smoked oyster.
Laugh, grunt, comic dialogue,
Caviar floating by on crackers.
"Every Sunday he burns my waffles,"
          Hostess giggles in the kitchen.

Host registers me with a wave.
Hostess could be his daughter.
Talk is trusses, beams, gleaming boundaries,
Ordering interiors inside out.
Goal is advantage the warehouse,
Leverage the clouds,
Return to the Tower of Babel.

"Wooden counter tops make me wanna chop,"
          Admits a passing debutante.

3.

The gathering thins at 11 o'clock.

On a granite counter,

An ashtray shaped like a heart.

High fives and goodbyes

In a stone foyer

Scented with gardenia water.

Host hugs the senior partner.

The door chains up.

The Transamerica

Glows high on a bookshelf.

"We'll move if we have children,"

      Hostess whispers from the kitchen.

Her

He waits in the bedroom. Windows face the street she takes to find him. A Dutch Elm on the front lawn reaches into Heaven. He lies across her bed, watching for headlights.

He hears the usual: children being hustled off the street by parents. There are protests. He smells macaroni and cheese on a neighbor's stove. He is relieved their day has ended. The children think they own the street—they mark the sidewalks with colored chalk, bounce balls, ride bicycles over the asphalt. But when the sun dies, they surrender claim. He owns this corner of the dark world.

He likes the house without light, without sound. He needs the street empty, the house black. The only light he wants is her light, the only sound her sound.

Light enters the room, fades. A car door squeaks, shuts, then footsteps over the dead leaves. He hunts through windows, sees her take the walkway, her face moving through moon and stars.

The Voices of Leaves

There is truth in
The voices of leaves
Cracking and breaking

Beneath my feet
When I take my walk
Just before dusk.

I should perhaps
Avoid this path
And save these voices

For the feet of children
Racing over the earth
Into the sun.

At the Stanford Park

The sun detonates the end of August.

Date palms explode the sky.

A boy with breasts backstrokes the pool.

Waves slap the greasy tiles, spray the Futurestone.

A dove sips from a crack.

Speedo man sweats jumping jacks.

Marigolds wilt in courtyard boxes.

A forest blooms beyond the flowers.

Bikini hands lotion legs and shoulders.

She is Venus with lavender toenails.

A jet cuts the blue—the sun weakens.

Women study Venus through tinted glasses.

Men contemplate the silicon climate.

A wasp lands on my towel.

Newspapers and cloth slippers cover the ground.

A New York husband leaves his Boston wife.

He heads east, chasing yellow light.

A wedding balloon floats to the moon.

The ice plant closes its blossoms.

A breeze stirs a cyclone fence choked with ivy.

Behind the fence, a forest woman suckles her baby.

Giant oaks shadow us all.

Pool

Your pool's a blueprint for logic, earth
Measured, dug up rectangular, hauled away
To fill other holes. Pay dirt? Pool
Lacks sufficient horizon. It's safe,
Safe to look on water contained by tile,
Safer than ocean stretching and bending acres
Into dark blue futures. Formula for success:
Detach enough tap water, shape it, heat it,
Chlorinate. And don't forget circulation.
Depth deepens, registers on sky blue tile as
Black numbers. Chrome ladders dip.
Pool's no threat to ocean—shoreline doesn't
Shift, no rips, lacks currents to drag you
Places you'd rather not go. Pool sign warns,
No Lifeguard On Duty. Life preserving ring
Preserves what wants to float, yet lacks
Hand to make the toss, administer basic life
Support. Pepsi machine stands guard in lobby,
But only saves from thirst, never drowning.
Man dives into deep end, swallowed by water,
Gets splash where once was thud. Ripples make
Pool active, waves flood gutters. Makes
You forget displaced earth, dirt born here,
A field that once belonged.

The Marriage of Jeannette

That was some wedding up in Tahoe. Remember the church stuffed with brooding icons, the moon bluing the mountains?

At the reception, my ashtray leaked almonds. Gifts wrapped in silver and gold. A widow sent them a conch shell packed in Styrofoam peanuts—when the Best Man blew it, a C note flew out.

Jeannette? A crucified goddess. A femme fatale fallen. But you'd never know it the way that she waltzed. Everyone played along in the Grand Teton Ballroom. Remember the sea of green balloons? The hors d'oeuvres featured real crab meat.

I recall the Groom—victorious Caliban, in full dress. Bet he really tasted the springs back at Caesars Palace. Heard he found an old yearbook, fingered a phone book, called Jeannette up. He's Western Regional Big Shot for some big German copier. He told his Best Man he wants her pushing a stroller, washing trousers, breast-feeding his young.

Some day, when a mood overtakes her, Jeannette will remember that shell. She'll press it to her ear and cry when the world spells out her name, in waves.

The Woman in the Black One Piece

She crosses legs on the lounge chair,
Rests the book on her belly.
She smoothes lotion
Over arms and shoulders.
Funny how skin learns
Pink instead of copper.
Men sleep in Speedos
On the other side of the pool.
She knows she's invisible
Even to the man wheeling
A canvas cart, filling it with towels.
She contemplates the pool—
Her pain goes deeper
Than twelve feet under the board.
Axes have swung at her soul.

No Lifeguard on Duty,
Swim at Your Own Risk.

She treats wounds
With fantasy and chocolate.

She hears newlyweds
Giggling inside the Jacuzzi
And recalls the aftermath
Of a bedspread
Beside the picnic river.
The morning of stained glass promises
She believed, she really believed.
She slips on her glasses
And arrives at a Tuscan villa.
An Italian with a mustache
Parachutes into the heroine's life.
She studies a sky too blue,
Too deep to be real.

Man in December

Man wearing cotton robe
And rubber shoes
Canes his way to a lounge chair.
He sits, rests cane
On Futurestone.
Leg ejects from robe, tanning.

"Is that water cold?" he asks
         Girl in the shallows.
"Cold," she nods, "cold as Alaska."

His eyes shut. The sun
Feels as the sun felt
A thousand months ago,
When he was
Learning to swim
Sweet blue water
That burned like ice.

Retirement and the Home Boy

He refused to go overseas with his wife a second time because on that first trip he'd had a nasty case of diarrhea on a bus touring Lisbon. He hated to travel because it meant waiting around in airports and going on tours and tipping strangers. He hated changing dollars and hailing cabs and shopping for knickknacks. He'd refused to stroll with his wife to the Eiffel Tower because he thought thugs would frisk him and discover his money belt.

When his wife suggested a Mexican cruise, he pictured two weeks of hurricanes, heaving decks, and Montezuma's revenge. He said it was a good time for her to fly to Boston and visit her mother while he concentrated on gardening and home improvements.

She left him a month later for a blond steward she met in economy class.

Dining with Your Headshot

Tonight, I will dine with your headshot.
I prop you up against a wine glass
Then anchor your bottom with a spoon.

As usual, you sit at the head of the table.
You appear in a rare mood—
Blonde hair drowning your shoulders,

Lips full and parted. Eyebrows plucked
To form the hooks of question marks.
Candlelight tickles your visage.

I serve our favorite—duck a l'orange, wild rice,
Steamed artichokes. Perhaps you recall
Having me in the half moon of August

While bulbs of night-blooming cereus
Popped for the hungry tongues of
Moths. I have dreamt of us walking

A road in a town of cobblestones.
The only ones we knew were ourselves.
There were bogs, thatched roofs,

The scent of lamb and cabbage
Cooking in an oven. I notice you signed
Your picture "Love." The word is the faint

Child of a pen ruled by indifference. I will
Measure us with a yardstick over creme de
Menthe. I am sure we are shorter than the truth.

Fishman

We found a pink mountain. The mineral glittered in her hand. "What is it?" she asked. "Bauxite," I replied. Certain spots were soft, unstable, sucking like quicksand. We hiked until we reached a waterfall. We walked over water, stepping on stone islands. Statues surrounded us. One was half-fish and half-man: a man's head on a neck of gills. The legs were fins but the arms human. Fishman. She leaned against a statue of Jesus and cooled in the breeze from the falling water. "Careful," I warned. She smiled and said, "Paranoid." Something moved and I turned. Fishman wiggled. "He's alive!" I said. He wiggled free of his pedestal and swam through the air to reach her. She bent down to stroke. Fishman wagged his tail. She straddled his back. "No," I called. She grabbed his dorsal fin and Fishman dove down into the bauxite. She was gone. The waterfall stopped and the statues melted. The mountain flattened into a desert. The sky went violet. I found a mirror on a rock and brushed off the bauxite. I looked in—she was lying naked on our bed, holding a stack of snapshots. Fishman swam over and opened his mouth. His gills flared as he swallowed our lives, one memory at a time.

Love in the Library

Knee to ground, she begins
The innocent search

Through the Dewey Decimals.
Her tan hands bruise me

Without touching. Jeans say
"Guess" in a triangular patch.

Is that foreplay for "yes?"
She stands full of glances.

She dark eyes me, lips parting,
Body angling hourglass.

Her hips beg for wonder
As she saws me in half, quietly.

The Day after the Post-Production Party

The sun's a drug sun. It invents hope
In the smog sky. Summer was an angry

Lover. A brass clock glows
On the bookshelf. This bedroom functions

To worship—all her headshots are framed.
An ocean's out there, somewhere.

The staccato of traffic shakes the continent.
Her cats are with me; one hides under

The bed, the other snores on the carpet.
My walls are nailed. The TV snags

Invisible waves. The moon appears
Apoplectic over Hollywood. Her clothes are

Flesh in my closet. How do you
Corner grief, hunt it down?

Shiatsu

She was a venture capitalist from New York who made millions distributing adult videos. He was a B-type from Boulder she met during shiatsu class at adult school. After they'd paired up and his fingers worked their magic, she knew he was the one.

Two months later, they exchanged rings in a chateau outside Marseille. He threw a fit in the foyer when the concierge mishandled his golf bags. Up in their room, they swilled a bottle of brut. Then he shiatsued her in front of the fireplace.

When the fire died, she watched one of her videos and cried most of the night.

Transformations in Northern California

Investments secure us, can transform us from Democrats to
Republicans, make us worry as new owners about faded paint,
Dying landscape, pipes weakened by decades of renters and
Gallons of Liquid Plumber. Everything's relative, including my
Mother-in-law who holds the wedding pictures hostage and
Communicates constantly she's ready to become grandma.

What are you doing the next 15 minutes? Eating? Sleeping?
Meeting me at the corner? Sometimes I convince myself to take
Japanese or German at the local community college. Then
I'd have the edge selling American products, like land, trees,
Fishponds, the homes I grew up in. Funny how nostalgia soaks value,
Converts apparent ordinary to extra special. Do you ever drive by
Your old home and find new people parked, ignoring your lawn?
The Santa Ana conditions the grass dirty blonde by summer.

I face my lawn chair west, apply SPF 10, prepare to tan beneath
The sunblocked sun. Over fence, renters raise marijuana instead of
Kids. Backyard bonanza, without diapers. How much per bud?
They're usually introverted, make little noises like pulling hoses,
Turning compost, watering their 8-footers. It all smells organic.
I'm wondering if my wife's mother knows her only daughter's ring
Isn't 24 carat. I'm a fraud. My wife says love can't be spelled in
Gold. True, I've never seen a ring that big. Funny how our
Pink roses resemble backyard rags—toilet paper caught on branches.

Closet

A row of thin selves
Hangs in my closet,

Cleaned at the strip mall
Down the block.

Yesterday the magenta blouse
With khaki skirt.

Tomorrow the Navy suit
Or pants with a vest.

These skins on wires
Belong to someone else,

Someone who has become
A creature of joints

With yellow fat
Anchoring the heart.

I dated in those black dresses
Hanging in back.

Hooks are
Questions begging,

Who is this person
Alone on the bed?

Ironwood

Drive too fast and you risk missing everything,
Including the solo ironwood standing majestic

In the parking lot. The ironwood's long-term,
Isolated, in for the long haul with a view of this

Dying mall. A car moves over the blacktop, searching
For morning coffee. When wheels spin they sometimes

Give the illusion they're moving backwards, as if
The ghosts in the tires are trying to get back home,

Return to their rubber roots. You can't move something
Without risking history. Funny how vulnerable a

Car looks when its wheel is missing a hubcap, makes
You consider how easily pieces fall off, hit freeway

Rolling, take another direction, lost. Should we keep
Moving forward with missing parts, ignoring their

Contributions? Replacements seldom match up.
A sign advertises *Private Road* across the street from

The mall. That path demands a special sticker for your
Bumper: peel backing off, stick on, stuck forever.

Sprinklers shoot orgasms over plants planted on islands
Floating between concrete and asphalt. Man-made islands

Display a heavy-handedness, like the oil company atolls
Off Long Beach coast—they require more than just ocean

To define them as things cut off, surrounded. Coconut trees
In Hawaii have aluminum bands around their bark to

Keep rats honest, prevent them from climbing up and
Enjoying the nuts. Those bands are wedding rings,

The trees in love, palm fronds touching.
The ironwood? Only it knows the meaning of alone.

Chasing the Moon

It's raining again,
Even raining out at sea.

The seasons are confused.
Winter knew only drought.

Spring brought the weeds.
Even the weathermen wonder

If it's really summer.
The sun hunts the clouds

And the clouds
Hunt the sun.

Light wants dark.
Dark wants light.

Everything's taking turns
Being pursued

And then
Pursuing everything else.

I remember the moon

Chasing me

When I rode

In the back seat

Of my father's Olds.

Now I wait for the moon

To rise in the twilight

To chase it for words.

New Jersey Suburbs at Dusk

Couples embrace in the community ballroom. Single girls not asked to dance giggle confessionals—the one as tall as a Dutch Elm peers over the dancing couples, winks at the married mailman.

Haul in the barbecue coal, burn it. Swing in the backyard hammock. Telephone poles crucify intentions. Fireflies fat, full of light, become flying flashlights that ignite grandparents' faces. I sweat pearls of beer under a giant clay priest pointing west to California from his knoll above the expressway.

Neighbors laugh, cough, conduct seizures of sneezes during family reunions. Refrigerators open. Many arrest memories raking leaves or pouring circular driveways. Smell cement, fresh cut grass. Weekend bedrooms distill the silence. Fall asleep during commercials? We are our own best tortures.

Children play in patterns, claim victories over asphalt. Sun moans toward eclipse under neighborhood fences. Trees gleam various greens. A washing machine screams, caught in its final rinse cycle.

Wind is generous, samples wax on parked cars. Garage sales introduce neighbors to convenient museums. A minute is represented by a significant dot on a second-hand clock, depicts quick futures. The sun calls the long day, turns the ball over to twilight. Districts are powered by weekend promises. Girls bathe tonsils in street corner beer, tan themselves orange under the burning halogens.

A brown bag rolls like a tumbleweed across the pavement. Boy becomes his father behind the wheel—he fears cul-de-sac traffic through a rearview mirror covered with webs. Wind whispers whiskey and soda. A dove bears down on a Styrofoam cup, swallows greedily, like a bird of prey.

Who inherits the metal? A neighbor watching college football fingers his sandwich made hours earlier from dolphin-safe tuna. He bites into mercury. A jagged spear of light hurls into an alarm bolted to his living room wall. Downtown, his wife enjoys her manicure.

A divorcee jogs her bottle blonde hair and dog beneath white lace clouds. Imagine leaning head into sink washing in yellow streaks? Fathers and sons allow her to enter their souls—she splits nuclear families apart with store bought light. Overhead, clouds hemorrhage adulterous pink.

55

Cars display dents. Cats yawn on Astroturf doorsteps, preparing for night. Planes the intensity of Venus and Jupiter pretend to be orbiting light bulbs. Roofs cover the bald spots of owners.

Wind acts as a cushion for ghosts. Hear sirens? Earth could crack under the ambulance fog, spilling forth ancestors. I consider the fallout, the possibility of debris, and am happy for things decaying, fermenting in residential glamor, maintaining the suburbs through bitter routine.

A Long Dark Sleep

I have come out of a long dark
Sleep to find I own nothing, am

Nothing. My teeth? Gray pillars
Grinding. In the dream light

Of June, I taste blood
In a lover's kiss. We have

Bullet dialogue, heartbeats exchanged.
Where will I be buried, ashes

Scattered? The dead know
What I'm saying.

The world is out there making deals
While we continue to sweat

Under the bone-white sky.
I grease her day with attention.

Insomnia Birthday

Insomnia means being alone, exiting your bed
Incognito before your lover wakes up.
You can't force the Sandman to deliver, it's
Not like pizza. Insomnia is the place
Where things keep on working in darkness.
Streetlights complement moon, planets, stars,
Lighting sidewalk where nobody walks.
Why not last one home on block turn the lights off?
Natural and artificial combine to highlight
Wet streets, trees, even veins in my leaves.
Under moon, dog rolls over in doghouse,
Moans in his dream. Refrigerator starts purring
When its thermostatic brain says keep the
Cake cool. Is newspaper girl rubber banding
My morning news? VCR blinks the seconds blue,
Same pace as my heart. On Entertainment
Center, birthday cards review my years in
Recycled paper. Books flex titles on mantle.
Candles on dining room table are at the ends of
Their wicks. Train from San Jose whistles, picks
Passengers in the donut twilight. Candy canes
Stand in the basket where the house plant died.

I never get sleepy until that first bird chirps,
When the violet light challenges street lamps.
Tires make revolutions in drizzling streets.
Will newspaper girl remember the weather,
Wrap my news in plastic? Even when the paper
Gets wet, I never complain. Have you seen 4 a.m.
After a big rain? That's the best time to catch
Your neighborhood ghosts walking the blacktop.
You'll see them congregate under the streetlights,
Execute their march, then stop to reflect in the water.

Observations during Insomnia

Moonlight and shadow puzzle the floor.
Window blinds blind only when closed.

There's cool in the dark throat of the fireplace.
Sympathy flowers wilt on the table. A friend

In another city wants me to mail pain
Killers. My prescription turns illegal.

The tomatoes in the basket are still life
Ripened on the community garden vine.

Crickets give the night a heartbeat. Nocturnal
Animals bring blood to the backyard; hides cruise

Through eucalyptus. Dog lives with planets,
Venus at zenith over his doghouse. He ignores

Trespassers using the steady moon.
Pants hang in disarray on cat's chair.

Lover waits in dream for my return: last month
She risked everything for our son.

Flesh surrounds my pulse. Cat slinks to window.
Moon blazes forward, shadows the mortal hours.

At Half Moon Bay, San Francisco

I believe in the shadows of birds, wings
Full of dark angel, feathered arms

Gliding for beach. This is a movie,
The wings are frames flickering by.

The sun plays tragic hero, bleeds
To the sea at the bottom of the hill.

Boy on the dune watches birds
Fly in before the big rain,

His twenty-two waiting for beaks.
Birds move with one conscience,

Block pieces of sun, build
Fragments over the blond sand.

Ocean the temperature of love.
Boy triggers the shadows.

Now is history
As fast as the mind remembers.

Freeway March

On 280 to San Francisco, driving my insomnia north,
Fighting mergers in these opening rounds of freeway.

Wife sits in back seat, Mother-In-Law up front.
Steel rail keeps us from people heading south.

Typic is one human per car, steering empty
Seats. No penalty for being alone, no car pool lane

To make you feel guilty. Cowboy in Bronco rides the range.
Lexus woman yawns. I cough. Bob's Supply Co. van

Speeds up, passes. Some drive with both hands on wheel,
Hands at 2 and 10. Service is 10 a.m. How we separate deter-

Mines height of sky. Ceiling fogs. Mother-In-Law looks
Forward to "Russian goodies" after service. Wife wants roses

Sent to Great Aunt's home, not Mausoleum. Funeral talk.
Church is Russian Orthodox. Coats hang in back seat

Next to Wife. Umbrella waits in trunk. We pass flat tire,
Car jacked up, hazard lights, a man sprawled on asphalt

Shoulder. Remember the Good Samaritan? I worry about
32 p.s.i. in all my tires. We pass one another through air,

On air, on routine missions to air-conditioned offices.
Mother-In-Law mentions squirrels eating peanuts on

Fences. We watch one another through glass and mirrors,
Spill our coffee on the sunrise. Freedom means talk on

Phone, snap on clip-ons, shave with a portable, drink from
The stained walls of a mug. Blue signs advertise *Call Box*

Every 200 yards. Telephone lines loop over
280, wires joining voices. Mother-In-Law speaks

Birthday lunch, Van Gogh Show, realizing
Claustrophobia in the underground garage.

I remember Great Aunt's porch blooming roses, trellis a
Wall of orange blossoms. Lemon trees yellow and green.

Wife asks Mother if she's feeling cold. Mother-In-Law
Pulls on sweater. Look at all that traffic moving south.

From the back seat, Wife throws me a kiss in the rear-
View mirror —I catch it, carry it far beyond our exit.

Nútungktatoka

Material matters will be destroyed
By spiritual beings who will remain
To create one world and one nation.
Hopi Prophecy

Things spill out with frequency,

Especially childhood beatings and secrets.

Remember when you used to lie

On your back on grass

And play with the clouds?

    Now find a seat on the salt train and

    Watch your face get pulled by wires across a cloudless sky.

These gray heavens

Shower my accomplishments,

But beyond the quivering magnolias

The ocean laughs. I fill my life with little miseries,

Trying to disguise surface weaknesses.

Does what's on the inside trickle out

And spill into morning coffee,

Me drinking my reflection

Again and again?

See the skeletons dance their dance for flesh.

They move like the rivers move

Beneath this city, quiet and desperate.

Overhead, a plane does its mock planet routine.
The moon pulls our bodies over walls,
Joins our shadows. Horizon bleeds, spills twilight.
The sky? In pain.

> I hurry my crab meat self
> Over the bones of the forgotten,
> Foraging for things I don't understand,
> Things that won't resist my claws.

Kung Hei Fat Choy

1.

"Kung Hei Fat Choy, Kung Hei Fat Choy," Mr. Lee says from beneath hospital sheets, "Happy New Year!"
"Not yet, " I correct.
"Almost, Mr. Fong, almost," Lee pleads. "Only three hours more. Then, the Year of the Dragon."

Sure. Three hours from them carving another year in my marble. Years link up like a cord of porkloin sausage swinging behind storefront glass. Outside, in twilight Chinatown, gunpowder thunders its execution of the dying year.

It's about time for that stainless steel bedpan when I consider my lungs. I'm waiting for cold, probing metal to bleed cherry blossoms from me. I've become a harvest of flowers, for doctors.

2.

At eight a.m. my gurney comes. I roll through a tunnel, past doors with tiny windows. Taking a ride. Silk palms sway from planters filled with filters. Smells menthol. I cry from Dragon eyes.

How many seconds could just one more cigarette extract?

Emergency keyboards static. I'm heading for something beyond pure chainsaw. Then the wheels stop. I squirm on the gurney. A nurse stands in the doorway, a nicotine halo circling her head.

The Longest Day of the Year

Here is the ocean,
This great blue

Melting the coast.
A squirrel finds an apple

At the high tide line,
Runs toward a beach house

Mouthing its prize.
Seagulls huddle on shore

Pretending to be decoys.
Today, we do not age.

Men pushing fifty
Play horseshoes in the sand.

Bikini girls
Play the shallows—

Legs, arms, hands
Honeyed in sun

Beckon from the oily water.
I hear ghosts speaking in waves

But can not understand
What they're saying.

They speak all at once,
Like a room full of people

Chattering at a party.
A set becomes music

And then I recognize
Rachmaninoff.

Winter at Carlsbad Beach, California

The tourists have fled
After an onslaught of wind and fog.
Kelp stretches in tangles,

Strangles the sand.
Seagulls huddle
Outside a seaside condo.

Behind a window,
A woman sits at her table
Playing solitaire.

The ocean is missing its surfers—
It is its own sky,
Dark gray and heavy.

A boy throws a stone at the water.
To the south, a power plant
Sends yellow blooms

Through its tower.
I smell burnt diesel and metal.
A jellyfish has been deposited

At the high tide line.
Here is a body of clear rubber
Etched with blue and purple veins.

This casualty requires no x-rays;
I cup my left hand
And dig a grave.

A man with flexing pole
Pulls a fish from the shallows.
The gold tail flaps onshore

As furious as a puppy's.
He slides his blade
Through a brain drowning in air.

Now there is blood on the sand
And a man bent over a bucket.
I genuflect at the edge of the continent.

At the Hong Convalescent Home

I sit on a bed by the window
Smelling Clorox and Pine-Sol.
A bouquet of silver balloons
Shines on my bookshelf.
Mr. Wigton, my latest neighbor,
Snores through his feeding tube.
Those are diapers and flowers
Piled on his counter.
Nurse Debbie delivers
Chocolate pudding in a paper cup.
I study the violets.

> I see eyelids
> Struck by moonlight
> Flutter like wings.

I remember my subscription
To *Life*, smoking pipes,
Wearing a jacket and slippers,
Knee bends before ten,
Calculating taxes.
There was a woman in a purple dress
Who smiled at me, really smiled.

My second son gets in tonight
Arrives with his second wife
Soon after midnight.
At twilight, May Hong makes
Jell-O, fries, chicken pot pies.

> I hear cries
> Just before
> The souls go.

My teeth ache for red rare meat.
I watch Queeny the gardener
Butcher elms in the courtyard.
He chainsaws limbs,
Hacking off parts,
Then stacks as wooden blocks.
I suck chocolate
Through a straw.
Nurse Debbie bends over,
Adjusts the wheels of my stroller.

View from a Library

Sometimes it's enough to
Sit and watch the broken,

Survey hubcaps circling on
Foreign cars and pedestrians

Crossing blacktop for bus stops.
Hear honk? Impatience paints

The street. There's patience
In the dotted white lines, our

Divided kingdoms, narrow
Empires running parallel.

Rap blends with country,
Pleasing five p.m. shadows.

I want sleep to roll over me
Like clouds, fat white walls.

Sorry I forgot to make Japanese
Rice, steaming hot pot, twenty-five

Minutes of flame, a burned
Match, an infinitesimal

Increase in kitchen temperature.
Outside, before six,

Drivers work the lanes
Employing reflex action—

Knee jerk instinct repeated in
Offices, meetings, motel beds,

Racing for reds and yellows,
Jack rabbiting a series of greens,

Some limping home
On automatic habit

Others heading for greasy
Pay phones at service stations.

At least we have roll, the
Safety of dead end streets,

A question of time, miles
Between library and home.

Palo Alto Wetlands

Men living in the Palo Alto Wetlands use disposable diapers to keep themselves warm. Their campfire rages across the street from the city dump. There's that smell of newborns. Cold wind threatens from the south. A moonless night discourages clouds. The top half of the world has blown off, letting in the stars. Men wrap diapers around their shoulders, like grandmothers with knitted shawls.

Just Before You Die

Just before you die
The ocean will recede,

Exposing the reef.
Birds will fly

Into the sun.
There will be

The smell of flowers.
The sky will darken.

Then you'll hear a noise.
At first you'll swear

It's someone blowing
A horn, kazoo, or trumpet.

Then you'll realize
That's not it at all—

It's really the sound
Of a baby crying

As it leaves the womb.
Hands will surround you

As you scream back
Into the world.

Fall on the Coast

The sea is rising. It resists El Niño
To remain choppy and cold.
Palm trees drink the breeze—

Their trunks sway like drunks
In beachfront parking lots.
The blue tower

Is missing its lifeguard.
These waves leave no room for surfers;
They fold in on themselves

Before drowning stones and shells.
A blonde wearing a green thong
Runs in and out of the shallows.

Race walkers race up from Carlsbad.
They pass a sleeping bag
And a man performing yoga

For a roosting seagull.
A crowd huddles on the coast.
Helicopters appear from the south.

Someone has disappeared
In the hypothermal water.
The anxious tide narrows the shore.

At the Art Institute of California

It is 6 p.m. in San Diego,
Minutes before I must teach.

The dusk blooms
A sunset that reminds me

The world is more than
Men and women

Hustling for evening coffee
Worried about children,

Babies to be,
Rents and mortgages.

The earth lives
Beneath the concrete and asphalt

We use to civilize souls.
The boundaries of

Water and sky
Break bread with the ghosts.

Reruns

How many dreams haunt your parking lot?
I hold my breath whenever I walk backwards,
Back to Hula-Hoops, rocking horses, and toy
Soldiers. Let umbrellas cover the sun, I'll swim to
The deep end. Daddy filled the pool with weeds and
Blood. I'm always stroking into television,
Diving for tears and laughter. The sun
Lives on the small screen. Boxed life. Nuclear
Fathers. A woman appears, advertising tires.
That warms the tubes. Hand on screen, I test sex
Under glass. She winks then wrinkles when I adjust
The vertical. We could be lovers, best love
Imaginable, but imagine her in fifty years—probably
Dead like me. Faces terrorize the glass, a rerun
With trains and girls and men raising rifles.
Someone on the train dies. In real life only the
Conductor survives, retires near Reno. I wonder if
It's all a dream. A yellow cat waits behind the door,
Wants to pounce on me like a tiger.
I could maybe tolerate that cat if he used this
Miracle litter being advertised again. Sometimes
I could slip a knife behind my eyes,
Scrape away the residue of childhood viewings.

Brother

A man
Who is my brother
Sleeps on the lanai.

He has become
The age of the father
I remember

From summers
Spent on Moloka'i.
But brother's snores

Are certainly
More ferocious.
He stretches

In his dream
Under a mosquito net
Until his ankles crack.

The Mark of the Ass

Big brother? Under our dining room table, busy. His fingers punch a black crayon against a pad of paper. He's drawing giant 3s. In private. He tells me they're asses. Whose asses? I ask. Everyone's, he answers. He draws fast, one ass a page. When he does more than half the pad, he stops. Your turn, brother says. He hands me the crayon. It's naked—he tore the label off and the point's worn down.

I'm not worried about getting caught. Mummy's gone. And Daddy's out on the lanai, drinking. Drinking and laughing. With the blonde lady. His arm's around her shoulder. You can hear them through the screen door. Now she's rubbing his neck.

My first ass? Weak. It covers only half the page. Brother makes a face. I try again. This next one's stronger. I move on, asses getting bigger, blacker. I kill the pages. My hand hurts doing the killing thing. Brother watches. I go faster and faster, pushing down harder and harder. The crayon bleeds. That's right, ruin the pages. My fingers ache but I won't stop. I fuck the pages, fucking them black, fucking them with the mark of the ass. It feels hot inside my belly and chest.

When I reach the last page, I push hard, slow. The black loops are huge. Filthy. Brother smiles. Then he takes the pad. The crayon's almost gone. I follow him into the kitchen and he buries our asses in the trash, under empty cans, bottles, and sour milk cartons.

Brother chases me outside. I run for the swings, running toward the grass, racing past my father.

How Much of What We Talk

How much of what
We talk
Is not for the lover
But the father
Who listens
Through the phone?
He calls me
By my brother's name.
Why did I always
Do worse
After his criticism
Than better?
Listen? He never listened.
His ears were
Too big for his head.
Mother cooked safe
Things—boiled eggs,
Buttered toast, Sanka with milk.
I rebel by killing me
A little at a time.

There was a time
(The 60s, I think)
When all I was
Was a peanut on legs.
I am the same legume,
Only smaller,
Craving love
After years of chaos.

View from the Second Floor

The hospice light is flawless.
The steel in my room gleams.
Gold embraces the linoleum.

Outside, butterflies tease the bougainvillea
With tongues.
The eastern hills are green.

Crows fly by without faces.
A red hawk perched on a fence
Devours a pigeon.

The wind carries the smell of blood
Through my screen.
Pine trees have fallen from last night's storm—

They lie helpless in the next lot,
Their roots burning in the sun.
These trees have joined me on the horizontal,

A level where the body
Can be easily poked and prodded.
This place breeds vertical nurses,

Transfusions, doctors whispering
In doorways. A white coat photographs me
Nude on my canvas.

I am a shutterbug's delight,
A deconstructing subject.
The lens blinks my mortality.

At 33,000 Feet

A gray wing vibrates the sky
Between California and Hawaii.

Below, the ocean corrugates.
The shadows of clouds

Float the purple surface.
There are ghosts in the water

Whispering about us
As if they know who we are.

An island looms like a continent,
Its volcanic cone

Rising above the clouds.
I am almost home.

Storm Birds off Oahu

Storm birds off Oahu circle clockwise,
Then counterclockwise over the cobalt sea.
Today I swim past the reef
Into the deep water where the waves are built.
Everything pretends to be as it was—
        the swells promising shore break,
        the surfers powering boards through the break zone,
        the prayers for yesterday's waves.
A turtle rises, gasps, fills its lungs with rainbow air.

I see the fields burning on the North Shore.

We hiked to find Old Hawaii.
I remember you looking down
Over Oahu's burning acres of cane
And the abandoned pineapple fields on Moloka'i.
The clouds were white flags on a blue sky.

The path I cut through this ocean
Will be erased, the ripples giving way to the reflection
Of hotel towers, intersecting mountains, cane-smoked sky.
But our footprints are messages left behind:
        kisses in the red earth.

Black Point, Oahu

I sedate
In the coconut breeze,

Ponder the hum
Of runaway ocean.

Men test the shallows
With spears—they

Stab at shadows
Then poke and prod holes

Beneath the surface.
The men are

Stick figures, bending.
The sea is a canvas of tortures.

The beach is missing its
People. Mansions at Black Point

Pretend to be human.
They crowd the soft bay,

This skinny shore.
Waves slap the sand,

Repeating yesterday
And the day before.

The water fills
With pleasure boats.

A sharp white sail
Severs water from sky.

Moloka'i Beach House

The interior doors
Have been torn off their hinges.

Lauhala mats cover the floor.
Papayas and guavas

Wait in a wicker basket.
Tiki gods flank the TV.

Tools of the kitchen have become
Ornaments. A copper cake mold

Is mounted over the stove.
A platter with hand-painted fish

Hangs off the wall.
The storm windows are open.

Coconut trees on the beach
Are a curious bunch;

Some bend for the sun,
Others resist it.

Kona wind carries
The scent of deep ocean.

Islands huddle
On the southern horizon.

The sea is a mirror—
It sends reflections into the house.

The gods smile
As the walls dance like rivers.

Love from a Distance

He loved her but she married another man and moved to another island. He often drove to the cliffs and stared out at the hump across the channel.

He ran into her on her island. She'd been married two months and worked at the car rental. When she passed him his keys, their hands touched and there was a moment where anything was possible. Then she told him she was expecting a baby.

He asked for directions to his hotel. The highway skirted a pineapple field that stretched to the horizon. He was tempted to stop but the fruit was too small and green.

As he drove east, he prayed the baby would never be born.

Moloka'i Budget Vacation

The lawn is full
Of weeds and stumps.

Trees have been
Beheaded here.

Two dogs sniff
An eel carcass—

They choose sides,
Stretch it like rubber.

The smell of death
Defeats the gardenias.

My plywood shack
Overlooks a harbor

Stuffed with lobster shells
And liquor bottles.

The beach east
Is thin and beige.

The shallows to the west?
A minefield of sting rays.

Aloha, Lili'uokalani

Queen Lili'uokalani, where is our aina?

My memories are a mixture of slack key,

Plumeria, and Kona wind in the trees.

I measure the trades with a desperate tongue.

Kapiolani is a park. Kaiulani is a hotel.

It is no longer enough to watch

The winter tide test the persistence of shores.

Lili'uokalani, do you see what I see?

Do you see my hotel uniform drying

On a balcony overlooking H-1 Freeway?

Honolulu windows burn a thousand suns.

But it keeps raining out at sea.

The rain comes warm, unexpected.

Do you, Queen Lili'uokalani,

Hold back tears for what you lost?

Did you carry your grief into heaven?

Paradise falls to us in pieces,

Pieces governed by the highest bidders.

Their blueprints cover sacred land with walls.

Walls to protect investments.

Walls to exclude the less fortunate.

Walls to keep Hawaiians out.

Kapus make Hawaii a land of strangers.

Beach access is a narrow path between estates,

A strip of crushed coral and flowering weeds.

Sometimes I see the rich dipping their toes

In the chlorine safety of oceanfront pools.

Dear Lili'uokalani, Hawaii is fee simple.

Hawaii is fair market value.

Hawaii is for sale and already sold.

A shadow falls on Iolani Palace.

Now Kalakaua is an avenue

Ruled by stoplights and crosswalks.

Likelike and Kamehameha

Are remembered only as highways.

The majority encourages progress.

The majority is no longer Hawaiian.

Kahala Beach, 2001

I am alone
On a thin beach
At Christmas.

The mood is summer,
The shallows
The temperature of blood.

Bodies glisten at distances,
Me on a strip of sand
Watching flesh tan

On alternate strips.
Tourists struggle
Over the rocky coast—

They dip and jerk
Like marionettes
In a school play.

The sea smells
Of weeds and salt.
Naupaka bushes

Green in the sun.
The sand moves as I move,
Shifts to accommodate.

I feel beached,
Marooned in mid-life
With Coppertone bottle,

Wet trunks and cotton towel.
Breakers pound
The wall at Black Point.

Mansions are jaded
By repeat performances.
The lava glitters with rooms.

Punahou Reunion

For the Class of '73
And in Memory of Cecily Mayne-McClay

Here are the sterling lawns and tropical
Gardens that once belonged to us.
Love was discovered and hearts broken
As plumeria bloomed and fell.
Hear the whisper of ghosts?
Our history's here, from the coral walls of
Old School Hall to the stone steps of Pauahi.
Remember Homeroom Swim Meets,
Canteens, learning to cha-cha-cha in the gym,
The day Bishop Hall went down?

Punahou became our teenage outpost
As Cooke Hall's gable clock
Counted our days remaining in Eden.
The Land of Nod was beyond
Walls of night blooming cereus
And a three ton standing stone
Guarding the entrance. I saw
A rainbow arcing over Griffiths Hall
That spilled into a boulder on Rocky Hill.
Remember two scoops of rice and gravy
For lunch, your booth at the Carnival,
Field trips, Baccalaureate Sunday, the Prom?

Tiny yellow leaves from monkey pod trees
Rain down on campus like confetti.
There was a night not so long ago
When we stood shoulder to shoulder
Draped in maile and pikake.
The future was just past the footlights,
Through the double doors of the HIC.
We sang our final rendition of "Friends"
With more conviction and passion
Than at any practice. It was as if
We finally understood the words
And the memories we shared as a class
Flashed before our eyes.